Original title:
Island Dreams and Ocean Tides

Copyright © 2025 Creative Arts Management OÜ
All rights reserved.

Author: Sebastian Whitmore
ISBN HARDBACK: 978-1-80581-619-5
ISBN PAPERBACK: 978-1-80581-146-6
ISBN EBOOK: 978-1-80581-619-5

Call of the Siren's Tide

A mermaid sings while I snack,
Her voice is sweet, my chips attack.
I toss her fries, she dives for gold,
This wave of snack is getting bold.

She flips her tail, I laugh aloud,
Claiming my chips; she thinks she's proud.
With every crunch, a fishy jest,
In ocean's court, I'm truly blessed.

Seafoam and Starlight

A crab in shades struts by the shore,
With tiny claws, it can't ignore.
He dances 'round, a beachside star,
While seagulls squawk, 'You're not bizarre!'

In seafoam light, they all sing tunes,
A chorus of laughter under moons.
The jellyfish bops and gives a wink,
I join the beat and hear corals clink.

Lanterns on the Windward Edge

Lanterns sway on breezy nights,
A dance of laughs and quirky sights.
Each flicker shows a silly face,
I trip on sand, fall from my grace.

The wind it howls, the lanterns blink,
A gusty gale sends us to drink.
The ocean laughs, the stars conspire,
The night's a riot, we never tire.

Hearts Adrift in the Current

Two dolphins race beneath the foam,
They giggle, splash, this is their home.
With every jump, they lose their breath,
They dodge a wave to flirt with death.

I throw a sandwich; they swim near,
To catch a meal, oh what a cheer!
Their silly games, my heart's delight,
In playful tides, we share the night.

Horizons of Discovery

A parrot in a pirate hat,
Squawking tales of treasure chat.
The coconut fell with a thunk,
Wishing it was a ship full of junk.

Seaweed salad on a boat,
With crabs thinking they can gloat.
Shells whisper secrets of the sea,
But all they want is to be free!

Dunes of Resilience

Sandy castles teeter tall,
Until the waves decide to brawl.
A seagull steals a chip or two,
While I sit here with my shoe askew.

My sunhat flew with great delight,
Chasing seagulls, what a sight!
The sunburn stings, oh woe is me,
But laughter floats as wild and free.

Shores of Soft Sighs

Waves giggling, splashing near,
Tickling toes, oh what a cheer!
Finding crabs in a race,
Who knew they had such a face?

A dolphin jumps, a splashy jest,
Trying hard to impress the rest.
I wave back, a silly grin,
As salty winds knot my chin.

The Treasure of Whispered Waves

Whispers from the tides at night,
Jokes about fish that took a bite.
A treasure map made of seaweed,
Leading to a trove of crabs, indeed!

A shark in a suit, how absurd!
Riding waves, it sings a word.
With laughter echoing on the sand,
I'll keep my snorkel close at hand.

Footprints in the Sugar White

In the sun, we dance with glee,
Making trails, just you and me.
Footprints like a wild parade,
Oh look, a crab! I'm not afraid!

My flip-flops flew, they took a dive,
Chasing seagulls, feeling alive.
Sand between our toes, quite the sight,
I'll catch you soon, you slippery fright!

Echoes of the Endless Horizon

Whispers roll from waves afar,
The ocean's tunes, a karaoke star.
We sing to shells, they come alive,
They laugh, they jive, they do the hive!

Sunburned noses, what a flair,
A toucan's laugh fills the salty air.
With each swell, we jest and tease,
Floating along like a pair of cheese!

A Snorkeler's Reverie

Bubbles rise like giggles loud,
I spy a fish in a glittery crowd.
Flapped my fins, gave it a whirl,
But ended up chasing a swirling pearl!

Mask on tight, what a sight to see,
Me bumping into a very kind sea bee.
It buzzed and laughed, then made a dash,
Who knew ocean critters liked to splash?

Sails Emblazoned with Dreams

We hoist the sails with tangled cheer,
Our captain's hat, askew, oh dear!
The wind laughs wildly, a playful tease,
Shiver me timbers, is that a sneeze?

With maps of ketchup and mustard stains,
We set our course through playful rains.
Our ship's a sandwich—what a delight,
Relax, it's just a food fight tonight!

Secrets Linger under the Stars

Whispers of jellyfish float by,
They giggle as they glide and sigh.
A crab wearing shades, quite the sight,
Is hosting a party, oh what a night!

Moonlight dances like a sneaky cat,
While starfish play cards, imagine that!
The night is alive with laughter and cheer,
While seagulls drop snacks, oh dear, oh dear!

Dancers Amidst the Waves

Turtles twirl, doing the cha-cha,
One lost a flip-flop, ha-ha, ha-ha!
A dolphin's got moves, zooming past,
With a splash and a wink, he's a real blast!

The fish line up to join the fun,
In glittery shoes, they dance and run.
A party so wild, it's hard to say,
Who's leading the dance? It's hard to weigh!

Spirit of the Tidal Pools

In puddles of treasure, crabs make their lair,
They wave at the kids with a pinch of flair.
Starfish discuss the latest cool trends,
While an anemone giggles, making amends.

A snail with a shell painted bright, oh my!
Slips on a banana peel with a sigh.
With laughter erupting, the tide rolls in,
The pools hold secrets that sparkles bring!

The Poetry of Shimmering Waters

The ocean speaks in splashes and sighs,
With frothy verses under sunny skies.
A fish with a poem winks from below,
As a clam writes a sonnet, steady and slow.

Seagulls recite with a caw and a cackle,
While barnacles drum on the hull of a tackle.
In the rhythm of tides, a quirky refrain,
The sea tells its stories again and again!

Beneath the Celestial Waves

Beneath the stars, we dance and twirl,
The jellyfish join, in swirls and whirl.
We sip on coconuts, laughter in the air,
As crabs do the cha-cha without a care.

Seagulls squawk like they know the beat,
While seaweed fans tap their leafy feet.
A dolphin plays tag, oh what a sight,
We giggle and splash in the shimmering light.

Castaways of the Heart

We packed our dreams in a rusty boat,
With sandwiches made of old, soggy coat.
Our GPS broke, we're lost at sea,
But who needs directions when you have glee?

A coconut hat and a fishing pole,
We're experts now, or so we extol.
With every failed catch, we laugh and cheer,
Castaways or kings, we have no fear.

Moonlit Reflections on Coral Sands

Under a moon that's shining bright,
We build sand castles, what a sight!
With shells as doors and seaweed flags,
We rule a realm where each joke brags.

The tide comes in, our fort's a mess,
But we raise our cups, no need to stress.
As waves tickle toes, we trade silly quips,
Creating legends of our ocean trips.

Eternal Serenade of the Sea

The ocean hums a tune so sweet,
As clams perform a tap-dance feat.
We join the chorus, our voices soar,
With fishy fans that cry for more!

With sea cucumbers as our stars,
We dream of fame, with laughs from afar.
In underwater cabarets, we smile wide,
As crabs juggle seashells, with style and pride.

The Song of the Ancient Lighthouse

A lighthouse stands with a grin so wide,
Chatting with ships on the morning tide.
Its voice sounds like a rusty old bell,
Singing of fish and the tales they tell.

With a wink at the seagulls flying high,
It tells them jokes as they swoop and fly.
"Why did the crab never share its dinner?"
"Because it was a little shellfish beginner!"

Chasing the Spray in Twilight

The waves paint the sand with a foamy trace,
As the sun starts to dance with a golden grace.
I chase the sea spray, slip on my feet,
Laughing and tumbling, what a funny feat!

Shells whisper secrets, they giggle and squeal,
Each one a joke, can you hear their appeal?
"Why did the ocean break up with the shore?"
"Because it found someone who had more in store!"

The Ebb and Flow of Memory

Waves wash ashore with a splash and a cheer,
Bringing back moments I hold so dear.
Like a prankster who hides, then reveals the fun,
Each tide brings a laugh, until the day's done.

Reminiscing of times when the gulls took flight,
Dressed up as pirates in the fading light.
"Why don't fish ever play cards in the sea?"
"They might get caught, it's just not their spree!"

Mapping the Heart with Driftwood

A piece of driftwood floats by my way,
It carries the whispers of a cheeky bay.
Marking my heart with its curves and twists,
A treasure full of laughter that simply insists.

"Here's where I hid my collection of jokes,
Right between the starfish and two wary folks!"
From conch shells it echoes, a tickle and rhyme,
Making me giggle, oh what a good time!

Tales from the Tidepool

A crab wore a hat, very cool,
He danced on the rocks like a fool.
The seaweed swayed in delight,
As seagulls giggled at the sight.

Starfish told jokes, oh so bright,
While clams joined in, feeling quite light.
A hermit crab painted his shell,
"I'm fancy now, can you tell?"

An octopus played hide and seek,
But his eight legs made him too cheeky.
He tripped on a barnacle too bold,
And fell in the tide, oh so cold!

So if you wander by this place,
Remember the creatures' playful race.
The tidepool holds joy and laughter,
In every bubble, life's hereafter.

The Sea's Gentle Embrace

A dolphin with shades, what a sight,
He surfed through the waves, pure delight.
With a splash and a twist, he would glide,
Saying, "Catch me if you can—come ride!"

A seal tried to balance a ball,
But instead, it tipped and made him fall.
He rolled on the sand, what a clown,
Waved to the whale, who blew water down.

The sunset painted colors so grand,
As jellyfish floated, taking a stand.
"We're dancing on waves, don't be shy!"
Said the fish with a wink of his eye.

In this embrace where the ocean sings,
Every creature dreams of silly things.
So join in the fun, don't miss the show,
The water's alive with a gentle glow.

Reflections on Water's Edge

A pelican pondering, what a view,
Reflected his beak in the blue.
He thought he was the star of the scene,
Until a wave splashed, and he turned green!

A crab scuttled by, dressed in flair,
With a glittering bow, oh what a pair!
It shrugged off the sting of the tide,
"Who says crabs can't have fun with pride?"

A fish in a tux, looking so sharp,
Attempted to play on a floating harp.
But he tangled his fins, oh what a mess,
All the sea laughed; it was pure excess.

At twilight, when laughter fills the air,
The creatures unite with a funny flare.
So tiptoe to water's edge, my friend,
Where giggles and splashes never end.

Stars Entwined with the Sea

A starfish declared, "I've got the moves!"
Under the moonlight, he busts grooves.
The waves clapped back in perfect time,
While fish joined in, making it prime.

A sea turtle waltzed, slow and grand,
While bubbles floated, making a band.
The crabs rolled in, creating a scene,
"This party's the best!" cried a porcine marine.

Anemones twirled like ribbons in air,
Their colorful dance a whimsical flair.
Seahorses joined, with tails intertwined,
In this watery ball, joy was defined.

So when stars light up the ocean wide,
Remember the giggles at the tide.
Dive in the jokes that never cease,
In this realm of laughter, find your peace.

Coral Kingdom's Silent Song

Beneath the waves, a fish does dance,
It wears a hat, and takes a chance.
A crab with boots, a turtle's laugh,
They sip on seaweed, by the giraffe.

A seahorse plays the ukulele,
While jellyfish sway, oh so gaily.
The octopus juggles seashells with grace,
In this underwater, funny place.

Starfish applaud with their five-armed clap,
As dolphins file in for a nap.
A clam's in charge, with pearls all around,
In this silly world, joy is found.

So if you're ever wishing to roam,
Just dive down deep, make it your home.
For laughter and bubbles fill the sea,
In the coral kingdom, wild and free!

Voyage of the Dreamer

A pirate ship floats made of cheese,
With rats as crew, take life with ease.
They sail on dreams, with sails of toast,
Heading to find a brunch-time coast.

The captain, a cat, with a gold earring,
Claims plunder's fun, but breakfast's the king!
With eggs and bacon, they chart the tide,
In a boat that bounces, they laugh and slide.

Their treasure map leads to pancake hills,
Where syrup rivers flow, giving sweet thrills.
With laughter in waves and joy in the air,
A voyage of fun, free from despair.

So if you're hungry, grab your hat,
Join these sailors—how about that?
On a voyage of whimsy, come one, come all,
To breakfast adventures, the silliest call!

Marooned in Solitude

A penguin alone on a desert isle,
Wonders why it has no one to smile.
He tries to fish, but they all just giggle,
As he trips and falls, what a grand wiggle!

An inflatable flamingo floats by,
It's wearing sunshades, oh my, oh my!
The sunshine beams down, as he takes a dip,
With a coconut drink, and a funny sip.

He builds a sand castle so very grand,
But the tide rolls in, with a mischievous hand.
It swallows his work, and washes away,
Leaving him grinning, come what may.

So marooned he may be, but quite the delight,
For laughter and joy are his guiding light.
In solitude's arms, he finds joy anew,
With a flamingo friend, making lemonade too!

Tales of the Nautical Wanderer

There once was a sailor, whose boat had a grin,
It sparkled at night, a real underwater kin.
With seaweed as sails, and laughter as fuel,
He traveled the waves, a whimsical fool.

His fishy companions were never quite shy,
With fins and with gills, they'd leap and fly.
A dolphin named Bob told jokes of the sea,
While crabs wrote his tales, oh what glee!

They'd stop for a snack on a mermaid's plate,
With cupcakes and sand, they'd celebrate fate.
With laughter resounding across the blue swell,
Our sailor found joy in each wave and each yell.

So here's to the wanderer, sailing so free,
In a world filled with whimsy, just wait and see.
With waves full of laughter, friendship, and cheer,
The tales of the sea are the best ones, my dear!

A Harbor for Wandering Souls

In a port not far from la-la-land,
Where mermaids dance with seaweed strands,
A sailor lost his socks one day,
Now they float like boats on the bay.

Seagulls squawk about their plans,
To steal our snacks and dance like fans,
A fish in trunks, quite all the rage,
Sipping seawater, he took center stage.

With pirates telling jokes so dry,
While dolphins giggle, oh my, oh my,
A crab in glasses, quite the sight,
Chasing waves till the end of the night.

So grab your hats, oh matey dear,
In this harbor, there's nothing to fear,
With laughter echoing through the tide,
Join the fun on this wavy ride.

Camouflaged Wishes Beneath the Surface

Bubbles rising like thoughts on a whim,
Where wishes swim, the lights grow dim,
A turtle wearing shades, oh so cool,
Says the ocean's just a giant pool.

Starfish building castles in the sand,
While crabs do the conga, so unplanned,
A fish with a hat, quite debonair,
Claims the tide is his secret lair.

With a flip and a splash, they dance below,
Playing tag with the waves in a row,
Mermaids giggle, their laughter rings,
Tossing pearls like the joy that it brings.

So if you're lost in the briny blue,
Remember this dance, it's calling you,
With heartbeats synchronized, you'll find,
That laughter's the anchor for every mind.

Enchanted Harbor's Call

In the mists where the jokes reside,
A lighthouse flickers, glowing with pride,
Where boats are really just seafood carts,
   And fish tell tales that tickle hearts.

The captain's hat is far too big,
He turns to jelly, like a dancing twig,
While parrots crack wise, a feathered crew,
   All aboard for the silliness brew!

With each wave that rolls and sways,
The seaweed wiggles, the sun's bright rays,
   Creating laughter that's oh so bold,
In this harbor where humor unfolds.

So come, my friend, leave worries ashore,
Let the sea's laughter open the door,
For beneath this sunlit sky above,
The waves share whispers of silly love.

Where Waves Whisper Their Secrets

Oh, the waves are gossiping today,
About clams and their pearls, in a flirty way,
A dolphin shows off his shiny bling,
While jellyfish float, doing their thing.

Seagulls dive down for the popcorn feast,
Stealing snacks like a furry beast,
And starfish high-five with eight-handed glee,
While crabs do the moonwalk—oh, can't you see?

A treasure map made of jelly, no doubt,
Leading to jokes they can't live without,
With waves that curl, giggles ensue,
A splash of fun, just for you.

So as the tide drips off the shore,
Join in the laughter—there's always more,
For in this watery world so bright,
The secrets of joy float through the night.

The Coral Kingdom Awaits

In a seaweed suit, I take my stand,
Fish as my pals, they all lend a hand.
Bubble parties pop, oh what a sight,
Jellyfish dancing, it's quite the delight.

Crabs with their claws in a shuffle groove,
Sea cucumbers trying to bust a move.
Sandcastles shake with a giggling charm,
As starfish strut, causing quite the alarm.

Turtles on surfboards ride with glee,
While octopuses play hide and seek, you see!
Seashells clapping to the ocean's beat,
The coral kingdom makes every heart leap!

Mermaids snicker as they braid their hair,
Fins flipping fashion, so much flair!
With every splash, joy bubbles and sways,
The fun awaits in the sun-drenched bays.

Waves of Forgotten Wishes

Once I tossed coins, oh what a dress,
But the seagulls swooped, it was such a mess!
They chuckled and cawed, what a parade,
As I waved my arms like a playful charade.

Crabs in tuxedos threw me a glance,
As seaweed twirled, oh what a dance!
I begged the tide for my dreams to be,
But all it gave was a splash of sea tea.

Starfish were sprawled on the warm, wet sand,
While dolphins giggled, forming a band.
They played my wishes — made them a song,
But by the end, they just pulled me along.

With every wave that crashed the shore,
I learned to laugh, oh what a roar!
In the sea's embrace, my wishes may fade,
But the laughter remains, a life well played.

Beneath the Sail's Embrace

I set sail for snacks on a bread-loaf boat,
With a jellyfish serving — oh what a gloat!
The wind whispered secrets of pineapple pie,
As I chased after dolphins, shooting through the sky.

Sails singing loudly like a creature possessed,
While seagulls squabbled over who looked best.
A clam in a cap did a fabulous strut,
As I laughed so hard, nearly fell in the rut!

Fishy crew mates took to the floor,
A conga line formed, everyone wanted more!
With every wave that rocked this old barge,
We danced on the deck, feeling so large!

The ocean sighed softly under the moon,
As I begged it to play my favorite tune.
It croaked back laughter — wasn't a tease,
In this sailboat of dreams, I found my ease.

Lullaby of the Coastal Night

As the sun dips low and the stars take flight,
The wave's gentle whispers sing me goodnight.
Sandmen gather, spreading tales so tall,
Of crabs having parties and fish who can crawl.

The moon plays peekaboo with clouds fluffy bright,
While the fish play tag, oh what a sight!
Oceans giggle with every soft tide,
As starfish waltz in the warm, silky ride.

Mermaids trade secrets, their voices like bells,
While the breeze carries stories of oceanic spells.
I snuggle in seaweed, my soft pillow rest,
While crabs hold my dreams in their tiny clawed nest.

So close your eyes tight, let the lullaby flow,
The sea is a comedian, putting on a show.
With each gentle wave, let your worries depart,
In this world of laughter, the shore holds the heart.

Heartbeats in the Estuary

A fish once tried to wear a hat,
But kept bumping into a floppy mat.
A crab danced with all its might,
Chasing a shadow that took flight.

The seagulls laughed from their high throne,
As the frog croaked on a soggy stone.
An eel joined in, playing hide and seek,
While the tide came in, again so meek.

With every wave, a new joke rolled,
A clam recounted tales from old.
Shrimp giggled, flipping in the sun,
Life's a party—we're just here for fun!

A whirlpool spun with a dizzy swirl,
As jellyfish twirled, giving a whirl.
In this crazy estuarine scene,
Laughter echoes where the fish have been.

Secrets Sway with the Palm Leaves

A parrot tried to share a joke,
But all the palm trees just bespoke.
With leaves that rustled, but did not speak,
Who knew that palms loved to critique?

The coconuts giggled from above,
Each one dreaming of finding true love.
They swayed to a rhythm, loud and maroon,
While crabs tap-danced to a beachy tune.

A hermit crab wore a tiny shoe,
Said, "I'm fashion-forward, how about you?"
His shell was shiny, a real trendsetter,
While the tropical breeze made it all better.

In this playful grove of swaying grace,
Secrets whispered, with laughter embraced.
The sun sets low, casting a beam,
And all join in—a palm leaf dream!

A Symphony of Shells

On the shore where the shells convene,
A clam played the drums, it was quite a scene.
The conch sang loud with its boisterous call,
While snails took turns, trying not to fall.

Starfish clapped, with five hands in time,
A star performer; they sparkled and shined.
A sand dollar joined, a mint of the sea,
Counting the laughs that drifted so free.

The seaweed swayed, conducting the choir,
As dolphins leaped higher and higher.
Each wave that crashed, a note in the air,
Composed by the ocean, beyond compare.

As dusk painted hues of soft pastel,
The shoreline danced, under the spell.
In this concert, both wacky and bold,
Nature's humor is pure gold!

Beneath the Shimmering Surface

Beneath the waves, a bubble burst,
A fish poked out, ready to thrust.
"Got a joke?" asked a shark nearby,
But the fish just blinked and said, "Oh my!"

Octopuses played peek-a-boo games,
While a turtle claimed it had ancient names.
"I'm slow," it said, forming a grin,
"Yet, I've the best stories from where I've been."

The anemone waved, wearing a crown,
"Join the party," it called, with a frown.
"Don't be shy; let's put on a show,
Underwater antics? Let's make them glow!"

With a splash and swirl, every creature sang,
As laughter echoed, the ocean rang.
So next time you dip, take a dive in wide,
Uncover the humor beneath the tide.

Driftwood Fairy Tales

Once upon a log, a seal wore shades,
The fish held a show, with glittering parades.
A crab played the drums, with style so neat,
And dolphins danced forth in flip-flop heat.

They built a grand castle, with sand and rocks,
A throne made of clams, and rulers of flocks.
The seagulls were jesters, with feathers in tow,
And mermaids sang songs of life's silly flow.

But the tide came in, washed their dreams away,
The seal slipped and slid, called it 'slippery play.'
Yet laughter rang out, as waves rolled the foam,
For in driftwood tales, there's always a home.

So let the tide turn, the laughter will last,
For stories of whimsy, in waves, are amassed.
In the salty air, with joy we roam,
Where every driftwood dream feels just like home.

The Painter's Palette of the Coast

The ocean's a canvas, a splash of bright hues,
Where crabs paint the shores in fantastic news.
Brushes of seaweed with colors so wild,
And gulls swooping low, like a playful child.

A shrimp with a bow tie conducts a fine band,
While clams sing in harmony, isn't it grand?
The waves roll in laughter, a splash here and there,
Synchronized swimming by fish in mid-air.

The sun drops a wink, as the canvas ignites,
Coloring the horizon with sparkles and bites.
A chameleon crab changes with every splash,
While octopuses twirl in a watercolor dance.

So grab your own brush, let your laughter flow,
Join the playful tide where creativity grows.
For on this shore, with humor alight,
Nothing is serious, it's all pure delight!

Beneath the Fronds, a Whisper

Beneath the green fronds, a secret is stirred,
A crab tells a joke, oh haven't you heard?
The fish roll their eyes, they can't stand the pun,
While starfish just giggle, oh what fun!

A turtle named Ted plays hide and seek,
With the seaweed as curtains, it's quite the cheek.
They laugh and they wiggle, with glee they recite,
As a wave rolls in gently, tickling their fright.

A shrimp writes a tale on the sand with a stick,
About a clumsy seal, who diving was quick.
But with all of his splashes, he turned quite the mess,
And all of his friends? They just loved the stress!

So whisper your dreams to the leaves overhead,
With laughter as soft as the sea on your bed.
For beneath all the fronds, there's humor in play,
Just listen so closely, it's a whimsical stay!

Sunkissed Memories

Oh the sun kissed the waves, in a tickling tease,
Where fish shared their secrets with bubbling ease.
A whale told a story, whilst flipping a fin,
And crabs wore their shades, like a fashionable spin.

Sandcastles rose high, with moats filled with cheer,
The jellyfish giggled, as they floated near.
They had beachside parties, with shells as their cups,
While the tide played a song, and the sun cheers them up.

But when the sun sets, the memories glow,
Of laughter and splashes, the joy in the flow.
With laughter like music, it dances on shores,
Creating a finish that everyone adores.

So hold on to moments, as fragile as shells,
For humor and fun weave the finest of tales.
In each sunkissed memory, let joy take a ride,
Where the waves tell the story, of liveliness wide.

Echoes of Distant Shores

Seagulls squawk in silly flight,
As crabs play tag from left to right.
The waves roll in with a splashing cheer,
While fish wear hats, oh dear, oh dear!

Sunny days send the flip-flops flying,
Pirate parrots just keep on trying.
They squawk, they squabble, in the salty air,
As mermaids giggle, too busy to care.

A dolphin jumps with a wink and a twist,
It offers a dance, you can't resist.
The treasure map leads to sandcastles tall,
Where buckets and shovels inspire a ball.

So raise your drink to the salty breeze,
And laugh with the waves that tickle the knees.
For here in the warmth, there's always delight,
With sunburned noses, we party all night!

Whispers on the Water's Edge

Under the sun, a sunscreen parade,
As beach balls bounce, and children evade.
Turtles in hats stroll along the lane,
While flip-flops squeak like they're going insane.

The lighthouse stands like a wobbly friend,
With a light that flickers as if to pretend.
Seashells gossip in whispers so hushed,
While seaweed dances, all tangled and brushed.

A fish in a tux takes a dip for a laugh,
With a wink and a swish, it's a stylish gaff.
The crab devours chips like it's quite the feast,
With giggles and grins, joy is released.

So join in the fun by the shimmering bay,
Where laughter and sunlight chase worries away.
We'll dance with the waves, oh what a delight,
With funny tales shared 'neath the stars of the night!

Serenade of the Sea Breeze

Here comes the breeze with a tickle and tease,
It pulls at my hair and makes me say, 'Geez!'
The waves bubble up, trying hard to compose,
 While sandcastles melt without any clothes.

A crab starts a band with a beat on his shell,
It's a raucous jam that will cast quite a spell.
The fish in the sea start to jive and to groove,
With bubbles of laughter, they spin and they move.

A seagull swoops down, stealing snacks from my hand,
And I laugh as I watch, it's my new hungry friend.
With sunscreen and chaos, the beach life is bright,
 As we sing to the tide with sheer pure delight.

So let's dance by the shore with the foam at our feet,
 And savor the flavors of summer's sweet beat.
 For every wave crash is a note in our song,
 With smiles and good vibes, we can't go wrong!

Mysteries Beneath the Waves

Bubbles of laughter float up from below,
As fish in tuxedos put on quite the show.
The octopus jazz plays a magical tune,
While bright jellyfish twirl under a full moon.

Anemones wiggle, all dressed up to sway,
They throw wild parties at the end of the bay.
Crabs in their shells try to dance like the stars,
While sea cucumbers sing in soft guitars.

Shells whisper secrets of treasures they keep,
As sea urchins grumble, still half asleep.
The mermaid's mischief brings giggles and fun,
With every splash made until day is done.

So dive in the waters, let laughter arise,
For the mysteries here wear giggles disguised.
With waters that sparkle, we'll splash in delight,
In the playful embrace of the ocean's bright night!

Festival of the Saturated Sun

Under the sun so bright, we dance,
Our swimsuits stretch in a silly prance.
With burgers flipping, and soda splashed,
The seagulls squawk, they're quite unabashed.

A kid with goggles, gets caught in a net,
He grins at the fish, oh, what a duet!
A volleyball lands on a sunbaker's head,
While everyone laughs, some lay back instead.

A cook shouts, 'Catch!' with a wink and a grin,
As a shrimp flies by, like it's here for a win.
The waves roll in with a playful shout,
Summertime goof-ups, there's joy all about!

When the fireflies blink and the dusk starts to hum,
We roast marshmallows while the crickets strum.
With the taste of salt and the scent of fun,
We cheer for the dusk; what a day we've spun!

A Calm Between the Storms

The clouds roll by, a strange charade,
Where raindrops play peek-a-boo, not afraid.
The weather guy grins, he's full of cheer,
"Stay indoors, folks!"—but we want to steer!

We find an umbrella that's full of holes,
It's perfect for a dance, making silly goals.
Puddles invite us, we take the plunge,
Splashing around, like we've lost our lunge!

A wave of whimsy in a muddy great fight,
With rubber ducks as our soldiers of light.
The skies might darken, but we don our capes,
Superheroes of laughter, with wacky shapes!

When the storm decides it's had enough,
We flip our umbrellas; oh, aren't we tough?
Tomorrow's forecast? We'll wet our shoes,
In a calm before chaos, we cannot lose!

Snippets of Salt and Seaweed

Drifting on a raft of potato chips,
We catch waves riding with funny flips.
The seaweed wiggles, calls out my name,
"Join the sea dance! It's fresh, it's the same!"

With jellyfish jigs and crab ballroom moves,
We throw a shrimp party, so much to prove.
A clam with a crown claims royalty soon,
While a fish plays the accordion—quite the tune!

Tangled in laughter, we weave through the brine,
In this wacky world, where the sun loves to shine.
The seagulls gossip and gossip somberly,
About the odd humans who dance so comically.

We pack up a picnic, with sprinkles of zest,
Playing tricks on each other, we love this fest.
The taste of the shore, a fantastic snack,
With snippets of silliness, there's no looking back!

Kites in the Coral Sky

Kites in the air, oh what a delight,
They dance like mad fingernails in a fight.
A red one goes left, but the blue one won't stay,
While a green one's tangled—hurray for ballet!

Kids run in circles, their laughter's loud,
As a rogue kite takes off, like it's feeling proud.
It dives for the sand, gives a poor kid a scare,
No worries, he's laughing, with wind in his hair!

The sun is a beacon, casting shadows galore,
A hot dog flies past; we couldn't ignore.
With condiments soaring like nature's big joke,
And ketchup cascades, oh, what a grand smoke!

Even the crabs join our whimsical fight,
Grabbed a kitestring, oh, what a sight!
With sand in our toes and joy in our eyes,
We twirl with the kites in this colorful rise!

Navigation of the Heart's Compass

With a map made of pie and a compass of cake,
I steer my ship through the waters to bake.
The seagulls, they squawk, claiming they're chefs,
While I'm lost in a haze of buttery breaths.

The tide pulls my line, it's a fish of grand size,
But I find it's a boot with mismatched ties.
I sail on, undaunted, my laughter a breeze,
For who needs a catch when you've got such cheese?

In a sea made of jelly with boats made of toast,
I laugh at my fate while they all seem to boast.
With each wave that comes, I just giggle and float,
Navigating love's currents in a marshmallow boat.

So here's to the journey, my compass askew,
With every odd twist, I find something new.
Though the waters are wobbly, my heart's all a-thrill,
In this comedy ocean, I'll sail where I will.

Celestial Dances Amidst the Surf

When the moon wears a hat and the stars have a drink,
They waltz on the waves, and I stop there to think.
A crab in a tuxedo performs quite a jig,
While the fish toss confetti from their underwater gig.

The shells all chime in, making music all night,
While seaweed sways gently, it's quite the delight.
An octopus spins wildly, with eight arms galore,
Making up for the dancers who just can't keep score.

My heart starts to dance with this whimsical beat,
As I join in the fun, feeling light on my feet.
The waves are all laughing, or maybe it's me,
In a tangle of joy, down below at the sea.

So whirl with the tide in this carnival deep,
Where laughter's the treasure and memories keep.
In the glow of the moon, all worries subside,
Join the dance of the stars where the surf takes a ride.

The Dance of Falling Leaves

Leaves twirl like ballerinas on a stage made of air,
While squirrels throw acorns, a nutty affair.
I trip on a branch, fall flat on my face,
As the trees start to giggle, there's no saving grace.

With a gust of fresh wind, the leaves start to flee,
In a game of tag, they're all faster than me.
One lands on my head, it's a crown, oh so bright,
But my royal attire is just a comical sight!

The colors are shouting, 'We're pure autumn flair,'
While I try to catch up, but I just can't compare.
They rustle and tumble, in the breeze, such a spree,
As I sing to the heavens, "Hey, leaves, wait for me!"

So let's dance through the chaos, a festival's on,
With each leap and each twirl, I feel more like a swan.
In this cacophony of color and leave,
We'll find silly moments; it's hard to believe!

Soliloquy of the Sea Breeze

Oh, the breeze has a voice that tickles my nose,
It whispers sweet secrets that no one else knows.
It flirts with my hair, and I answer its call,
Pretending to dance as I trip and I fall.

"Come chase me!" it laughs, as it swirls 'round my toes,
Pulling at my shorts like a child who just knows.
I giggle and chase, round the sandcastles tall,
While the tide shakes its head, thinking I'm quite the fool.

"Don't you get dizzy?" asks a wise old sea shell,
I shrug and just chuckle, "I'm here for the swell!"
The breeze tickles my cheeks and it blows me a kiss,
I twirl with abandon, for moments like this.

So here in this riddle of wind, sand, and sea,
I share in the laughter, oh breezy esprit.
With every gust comes a storm of delight,
In this playful escape, I embrace the night.

A Tapestry Weaved in Foam

A crab tried a dance, oh so grand,
With one claw in the air and sand on its hand.
Seagulls they cawed, laughing out loud,
As the ocean played host to the crab's little crowd.

But the tide thought it funny, a twist and a splash,
The poor little dancer, he fell with a crash.
He stood up all dizzy, looked quite around,
As waves rolled in laughter, a soft whooshing sound.

Then fish in the school did a jig on the side,
They'd copy that crab, oh what a wild ride!
With tails all a-flip, and gills in a whirl,
They made quite the scene, oh what a big pearl!

When night finally fell, the moon chuckled bright,
As crabs crawled home under starry delight.
The ocean grinned wide, with bubbles galore,
For dreams in its depths, there's always much more!

The Haven of Sandy Solitude

A turtle so slow had a plan oh so sly,
To bury his snacks as the tide floated by.
With shells full of chips, pretzels, and dips,
He thought he was clever, with no need for slips.

But a seagull flew down with a keen eye for treats,
And stole all the snacks, never caring for guilt beats.
The turtle just grinned, it was quite a grand heist,
He figured he'd share, hey, why not be nice?

Then a fish in a bowl, looking bulgy and round,
Joined in with a wiggle, oh such joy he found.
They set up a feast with the sand as their table,
And soon everyone came, all the sea was unstable.

With laughter and splashes and a friend in each flipper,
The sandy retreat turned into a zippy zipper.
As waves joined the party with a swell and a cheer,
This haven was lively, full of friendship and beer!

Lighthouse Dreams in the Mist

A lighthouse stood tall with a flicker that flashed,
But inside the crab captain felt quite outclassed.
He wobbled and bobbed under the glimmering light,
While the waves did a tempo, both silly and bright.

The fog rolled in thick, like a blanket too warm,
And clumsy old gulls began their own swarm.
They crashed into beams, with a caw and a bang,
All the fishermen laughed, till the lighthouse sang!

With lanterns aglow, they danced through the night,
While the seashells all clinked in a whirl of delight.
The crabs tapped their claws, keeping time so neat,
As the lighthouse spun stories of oceanic beat.

Then morning would come with all colors in view,
Yet those dreams in the mist kept the laughter anew.
With tides swelling high, and sun in their eyes,
They waved to the world, with smiles and goodbyes!

Crashing Hopes and Silent Shores

A dolphin once dreamed of a grand acrobatic,
But slipped on some seaweed, oh wasn't that tragic!
He landed with splashes, headfirst in the sand,
The laughter of fish echoed over the strand.

With a wheeze and a wiggle, he shook off his pride,
As his fishy friends giggled at the sight by the tide.
They formed a loud conga, all wiggling away,
A party had started; oh, what a fun day!

The crabs joined the merry, with their pinchers in sync,
While the waves kept on crashing, making them think.
That maybe, just maybe, it's fun to be free,
In this joyful mess flowing endlessly!

As the sun dipped low, and the colors went soft,
The dolphin leapt high, feeling proud and quite aloft.
For every small tumble, there's giggles and bliss,
In the realm of the tide, how could you miss this?

Deep Blue Daydreams

In a boat made of cheese, I float on by,
Catching the giggles from seagulls up high.
The fish wear bowties, they swim with flair,
While I sip my tea and pretend not to care.

A crab tells my fortune, it's quite absurd,
With a flip of his claw, I'm a millionaire bird.
My cat is the captain, he's just taking a nap,
As I sail through the skies in my crumpet-shaped ship.

The sun wears sunglasses, it's ready to play,
While waves dance like dancers on a bright cabaret.
The dolphins are trading their best jokes and puns,
As I rattle my teeth at the silly sea runs.

So here's to the laughter that floats on the breeze,
With a sprinkle of humor and a splash of the seas.
Let's toast to the nonsense that makes life so sweet,
In this world of oddities, oh what a treat!

Tales of the Wandering Sailor

Once a sailor set off with a shoe on his head,
He thought it was clever, but the fish all just fled.
With pranks in his pockets and maps made of pie,
He sailed through the spray while the gulls laughed nearby.

He tried to teach jellyfish to do a quick dance,
But they stung all his toes, and he lost his last chance.
The octopus offered him some magical ink,
But he used it for doodles, which made the sea stink.

A treasure of laughter was buried with glee,
With coconuts giggling beneath the tall tree.
He traded his compass for a slice of fresh bread,
Now he's lost but content, using crumbs as his thread.

So here's to the mischief, to blunders galore,
To sailors who sail but are never ashore.
With jokes in the wind, life's wonderfully wild,
In a boat of pure laughter, let's all be that child!

Whispers of the Azure

Whispers from waves are a silly old tune,
Each bubble a giggle, each splash a balloon.
The sky wears a frown, but the sea gives a grin,
As crabs play the drums with claws under skin.

The clam shells are talking, they gossip all day,
About the old sailor who danced in the spray.
With his socks on his hands and a smile like the sun,
He tripped on a seaweed and we all had some fun.

The fish threw a party, on seaweed designs,
With dancing sea cucumbers and wine made of brines.
The starfish brought cookies, they tasted so sweet,
And the sea turtles served them on the old reef street.

So let's raise a toast to the silliness found,
In the whispers and ripples and laughter around.
The ocean is quirky, a wild, jolly place,
Where giggles are currency and dreams find their space!

Shores of Forgotten Wishes

On shores made of marshmallows, I dance with the tide,
While wishes play tag with the crabs on the side.
The sand's always giggling, it tickles my toes,
As each wave brings laughter from the depths below.

The flip-flops are chatting, they've stories to share,
Of picnics with pirates and whales with bright hair.
The sun joins the fun, wearing hats that are wide,
As seagulls all cackle at the joy they can ride.

Shells whisper secrets of dreams from the past,
Of sailors who surfed on the waves that were vast.
But I only care for my snack of fine cheese,
As the beach offers magic with each gentle breeze.

So here's to the wishes that float by our feet,
To the merriment found in this life that's a treat.
With laughter as treasure, we'll gather and play,
On shores full of wonders, all night and all day!

The Secret Haven's Lullaby

In a cove where seagulls dance,
The crabs hold a waltzing chance.
Pineapple hats upon our heads,
While turtles snore in beachy beds.

With flip-flops flying, oh what fun,
We'll race the waves until we're done.
The sandcastles crumble in glee,
As we sip soda under a tree.

The coconut palms nod and sway,
As we try to sunbathe all day.
But sunscreen battles with the breeze,
And laughter echoes through the trees.

At sunset, fish start telling tales,
Of ships with sails and runaway snails.
In this spot, where silliness reigns,
We'll dance with dolphins, shake off the chains.

Tides of Time and Memory

The waves forget the tides they knew,
As we surf past pirate ships in blue.
The jellyfish moan about their plight,
While we start a conga, oh what a sight!

Shells sing songs of sandy cheer,
While lobsters giggle, bringing a beer.
The seaweed twirls in a happy spree,
And we've lost the map, but are still carefree.

Sand dollars grant wishes, or so they say,
As we tumble and roll in our sunburnt fray.
The spooner crabs high-five us, too,
And throw a party with ocean blue.

Caught in nets of invisible fun,
We'll fish for laughter, one by one.
With every wave, a silly surprise,
As the sea winks and giggles and sighs.

Driftwood and Distant Horizons

Driftwood chairs by the salty bay,
With seagulls making a ruckus all day.
The waves gossip with conch shells near,
As we toast with juice and shed a cheer.

Sunburned noses, what a sight,
As crabs attempt to steal our bites.
The starfish play hopscotch on the shore,
While we giggle, asking for more.

Fishy tales from a wise old whale,
Make us howl, as he tells his tale.
And the sunset brushes colors so bold,
The golden hour turns to laughter, behold!

As twilight whispers secrets untold,
Clams and clowns dance, gleefully bold.
In driftwood havens, we find our plot,
With beachy dreams that hit the spot.

Enchanted Currents of the Night

Under the moon with shades of fright,
The mermaids' giggles fill the night.
We play charades with a curious squid,
While a walrus sings, and our worries hid.

Starfish sparkle like disco balls,
As we prance beneath the coral walls.
In the starlit waves, we lose our fears,
And build a ship made of laughter and cheers.

Octopus chefs whip up a stew,
While we do ballet, just me and you.
The dolphins join, twirling with grace,
In this moonlit wonder, at a frantic pace.

The currents giggle, tickling our toes,
As jellybeans rain down, who knows?
With winks and waves, the night goes wild,
In this magical realm, we're forever a child.

Flight of the Shorebirds

A flock of birds in silly flight,
They crash and tumble, what a sight!
The seagull's honks, a loud debut,
As they fight over chips, not a clue.

They try to dance on sandy toes,
While taking turns at splashy woes.
With every wave, they take a chance,
On dodging surf as they prance.

Their leader yells, "Let's soar and swoop!"
But lands face-first in a gooey goop.
The sunset rays, a bright parade,
As they giggle and jump, still unafraid.

At night, they gather, tell tall tales,
Of lost souvenirs and stolen gales.
In chaos wrapped in feathers tight,
These merry birds, a comical sight!

Ebbing Echoes of the Past

Old shells whisper secrets bold,
Of fishy tales from days of old.
A crab in a tux, he struts on by,
Waving his claws like he's sky high.

The tide rolls in with a groaning tease,
Saying, "Don't forget your beach-day sneeze!"
Seagulls laugh, flap and dive,
While people trip, they just survive.

Old memories swim like jellyfish,
Stinging the thoughts one didn't wish.
With each splash and bubbly cheer,
You laugh at fears that draw so near.

Oh, the past, a slippery friend,
It tickles your toes, but won't quite mend.
So splash in pools of salty lore,
And let those echoes sing once more!

Ghosts of Tempestuous Seas

There's a ghost ship dancing free,
Made of foam and mystery spree.
With sails of jelly, it floats and spins,
As the laughter of mermaids softly begins.

Fortune fish with glittering scales,
Swim with pirates in silly tales.
They sing of treasures, but what's the catch?
A ghostly parrot, with a leafy patch!

Waves crash loud, in fits of giggle,
As ghostly crew makes the world wiggle.
A treasure map all torn and frayed,
Leads to a spot where jokes are made.

Sailing off with a wink and grin,
The sea's old secrets turn to din.
Haunting fun in the ocean wide,
With the merry ghosts, take a ride!

Moonlit Pathways on the Water

The moonlight glimmers like a wink,
On the water's face, where sailors think.
With fish that glow like disco balls,
They dance in pods, doing silly sprawls.

Under the stars, a boat goes round,
With mismatched oars that make no sound.
A crew of cats in pirate hats,
Plotting mischief with squirmy brats.

Laughter erupts as the fish get wise,
Ducking beneath the big moonrise.
A cat takes a leap, lands in a splash,
While the crew oohs and aahs in a flash.

The night drifts on, with tales to weave,
Of silly stunts, it's hard to believe!
On moonlit pathways, dreams collide,
With giggles echoing, the tides abide.

Starlit Lagoon Reveries

Under a sky with glittering stains,
Fish give gossip, ignoring their pains.
A crab wears a hat, oh what a sight,
Dancing all day, then sleeps through the night.

Seashells talk tales of the fish's chat,
Whales giggle softly, imagine that!
The moon plays tag with a sneaky breeze,
While dolphins do backflips with utmost ease.

Laughter rolls in with the comical tide,
Starfish juggle seaweed, full of pride.
Octopus chefs, they flip pancakes wide,
Feeding the sharks who try to hide.

In this lagoon, where silliness swims,
Nothing feels tough, and life never dims.
So join the parade of the eccentric crew,
Where each wave brings a chuckle or two!

Where the Ocean Meets the Sky

Up where the sea waves salute the clouds,
Seagulls wear sunglasses, strutting in crowds.
A dolphin pulls pranks, splashes with glee,
As he flips over crabs sipping their tea.

The sun slips down, but the fun's just begun,
Surfboards are sliding like fish on the run.
Sandcastles sway, but don't call them static,
For they throw wild parties, quite problematic.

Mermaids with banjos sing songs of delight,
While shrimp form a band, playing rock every night.
The tide rolls in, and the laughter erupts,
As jellyfish shimmy and sea cucumber jumps.

Here where the ocean gives kisses to air,
Every wave is a joke, floating everywhere.
So grab your flip-flops and dance on the shore,
In this land of giggles, there's always more!

Secrets of the Mariner's Heart

A sailor once dreamed of a fish with a crown,
Who told him the secrets of seaweed renown.
"Wear socks in the sea!" the fish began bright,
"For a pirate's surprise, oh what a sight!"

The captain just laughed, but gave it a go,
With mismatched socks, he became quite the show.
Mermaids all swooned, and the crabs started clapping,
As the mariner twirled, feet happily slapping.

His compass spun wild, with each twist and turn,
For laughter was gold that the ocean would earn.
Treasures were found in the jokes of the sea,
With the mariner dancing, and all of them free.

So sail forth with glee, on this voyage bizarre,
Where sea critters giggle beneath every star.
For in every wave, and each ripple of heart,
Lies a chuckle that blooms, an oceanic art!

Coral Castles in the Deep

In coral's embrace, where the fish like to dwell,
Live the clam and the snail, with stories to tell.
Sea stars wear pajamas, oh what a sight,
Playing hide and seek, till the morning's first light.

The shrimp throw a bash, with seaweed confetti,
While turtles do limbo, looking quite ready.
Anemones wiggle, with humor profound,
As octopus waits with charms all around.

Bubbles drift up like laughter afloat,
In a garden of corals, they dance in a boat.
Each wave is a giggle, each tide a surprise,
As the sea creatures prank with glee in their eyes.

Among these castles of color and cheer,
Where humor's the treasure, and joy's crystal clear.
Let's dive in the fun, in the depths of the blue,
In this kingdom of coral, with laughter anew!

Celestial Dancers of the Abyss

Beneath the waves, a fish named Fred,
Wears a tutu, dancing, never in dread.
He twirls and spins, a sight to behold,
His moves like jelly, all jellyfish gold.

A crab in a top hat claps with a cheer,
While octopus plays the accordion near.
They throw a party, with bubbles galore,
Underwater boogie, who could ask for more?

Anemones sway, keeping time with the beat,
While sea turtles tap dance, swaying their feet.
A dolphin leaps high, tries out a new flip,
Sweet moves in the ocean, no chance of a trip.

So if you dive deep, keep your eyes on the spree,
You'll find the true stars of the blue jubilee!
With every splash, a chuckle will rise,
In the depths of the sea, where humor complies.

Gentle Rhapsody of the Surf

The waves whisper secrets, as they roll to the shore,
Salty sea breeze tickles, who could want more?
Seagulls sing loudly, as if in a play,
Arguing over the best fish fillet.

The sand crabs are gossiping, all in a huddle,
Planning a party, but too scared to cuddle.
They dig tiny holes just for their fun,
While shells watch in silence, thinking, 'We're done!'

A kid with a spade starts a grand tower,
But the tide plays tricks, it's under in an hour.
With giggles and splashes, they chase the retreat,
Building more castles, a race for the feat.

Each wave brings laughter, a gentle caress,
It's the ocean's own rhapsody—nothing less!
With each bobbing tide, a chuckle ignite,
A symphony of joy, from morning to night.

Seashells and Hushed Promises

Seashells collected, a colorful thrill,
One whispers secrets, but none can keep still.
"I promise to tell you," it giggles in glee,
But it's really a conch, with gossip to spree.

A starfish beams brightly, thinks it's a star,
But forgets to shine while stuck near the bar.
It's sipping on seaweed, feeling so grand,
But alas, the tide laughs, pulling the sand.

Crabs dress in plaid, discussing their style,
One thinks it's a runway—come stay for a while!
They strut on the sand, with a waddle so neat,
Making all the fish chuckle, it's quite the treat.

So gather those shells, hear their quirky tales,
In a world full of laughter, where fun never pales.
Every whisper and secret in a rhythmic delight,
Tides of mirth rolling in, oh what a sight!

The Horizon's Gentle Call

A little boat dances, on waves it does play,
It rocks and it rolls in a comical way.
With each crashing wave, it giggles and jives,
The seagulls squawk loud, 'Look, there it thrives!'

A parrot on deck speaks with a flair,
"Tell me your secrets, I swear I won't share."
But it squawks to the fishes, "You'll never believe,
This captain thinks he can swim, what a reprieve!"

The sun sets like a painter's big splash,
Colors worry about making a crash.
With pinks and yellows, it spills on the sea,
A canvas of whimsy, oh let it be free!

So answer the call of the wide open sky,
Let the breeze tickle you, give laughter a try!
With every horizon that beckons us near,
Life is a jest, that we hold ever dear.

Sunlit Sands and Seafoam Rays

In flip-flops I race, like a crab in a spree,
Chasing the waves, oh how they tease me!
With sand in my sock, and sunscreen on nose,
I'm the beach bum king, that everybody knows.

A seagull stole fries, oh what a bold mate,
He squawked in delight, like he's won a great fate!
While I juggle my hat, it flies off my head,
It's a circus out here, let's call it a spread!

The sun's doing whims, playing peek-a-boo games,
I'm soaking up laughter, not caring for names.
As waves roll away, like a bad puppet show,
I tumble and laugh, just letting it flow.

We'll dance on the shores, with wide open grins,
And chase all the crabs, oh let the fun begin!
With jellyfish winks and a starfish's cheer,
Our silly sun frolics will last through the year.

Tidepool Reflections

Peering in pools, I see my big grin,
With a starfish waving, let the games begin!
Anemones bounce with a tickling sway,
Who needs a therapist when you've got this play?

A hermit crab scuttles, in someone else's shell,
Wishing I had one, who'd say "Oh well!"
I join in the fun, take a dip with a splash,
But slip on the slime, and oh what a crash!

The tide comes to tease, pulling me back,
"Hey, where you going? Don't lose your snack!"
With sandwiches soggy, I laugh at the sea,
This circus of waves, it sure suits me!

So here I will stay, amidst laughter and tides,
With friendly sea critters, where giggle abides.
In this vibrant bazaar, of foamy delight,
Where joy and mischief play, both day and night.

Celestial Currents of Calm

Looking at clouds, I see creatures galore,
A whale's tail, or maybe a playful boar?
I'll build me a spaceship out of driftwood and glee,
To sail through the stars, oh how wild it'll be!

Pulled by the breeze, my hat takes a flight,
Chasing its dreams towards the glowing moonlight.
With dolphins as pilots and seagulls as crew,
We'll sky-dance together, just us and the blue.

The waves will sing songs, all enchanting and bright,
While I try to tango with a ladybug kite.
With laughter all around, we'll twirl like a pinwheel,
In this wacky old boat, it's a wonderful reel!

At dawn we'll return, on a hammock of stars,
With memories etched in munificent jars.
So grab your imaginations, and let the tide steer,
For this cosmic adventure spins laughter and cheer!

Driftwood Journeys

On a log I journey, with an owl as my guide,
We'll surf the waves, in the latest tide ride!
A crab with a medal, my co-pilot so spry,
Keeps insisting we fly, while I just wonder why!

With a shell phone in hand, I call up the breeze,
"Hey wind, can you help with my driftwood tease?"
It tumbles and giggles, does pirouettes near,
"Ride like the waves, oh let go of your fear!"

Through rivers of laughter, we splash and we swoop,
I'm lost in the joy, like a clown with a troop.
The sea whispers secrets, of mermaids in dance,
While starfish throw parties, like an undersea prance!

So here on this wood, I'll sway with my pals,
With jellybean waves and some fancy red snails.
We'll sail towards sunsets, with a song in our heart,
For every driftwood journey is a laughter-filled art!

Waves Cradle the Stars

The moon fell into the sea,
By accident, you see.
It swam with a shiny grin,
And splashed the fish for a spin.

A crab wore sunglasses tight,
Dancing with the waves at night.
He said, "Life's a beach, don't you know?"
As seagulls joined in the show.

Starfish gathered for a chat,
Debating where all the snacks sat.
One said, "I saw a shell,
With pizza! It rang a bell!"

So, they laughed as tides swayed,
In this watery masquerade.
When dawn broke, they waved goodnight,
Planning for another delight.

Sandcastles in the Breeze

A castle built with jelly beans,
An architect with wobbly genes.
He said, "I need more frosting here!"
While squirrels cheered with a loud cheer.

Seagulls eyed the cookie moat,
One tried to take off in a boat!
But it flipped, causing a ruckus,
As sand flew up in a circus.

The flags were made from old beach towels,
Waving proudly with joyful howls.
A crab was crowned king for the day,
As laughter echoed through the bay.

But as the tide came to play,
Our castle was washed away.
"Let's build another!" we all cried,
Through giggles and the ocean's side.

Lost in the Embrace of Water

A fish in a hat quite snug,
Told tales of a smuggly bug.
"I lost my way to the coral ball,"
Said he while doing a floaty crawl.

Octopus wore shoes on each limb,
Trying to keep his style in whim.
He slipped on seaweed, what a sight!
Twisted like a dance in the night.

A dolphin jumped in with a splash,
Said, "Let's party! In a sea bash!"
With bubbles that tickled the toes,
We spun in circles and struck silly poses.

As waves rocked us, laughter swirled,
In our underwater, crazy world.
Not lost but found in all the fun,
We swam beneath the glowing sun.

Beneath the Canopy of Blue

A turtle in shades, cool and spry,
Called out to a low-flying pie.
"Why must you float, all round and round?"
He chuckled loud, quite ocean-bound.

The jellyfish glowed, giggling bright,
Dancing with laughter, oh what a sight!
They twirled their tentacles with glee,
Singing, "Join us, come float with me!"

Mermaids played hopscotch on reefs,
Stole shells from gulls, oh what thieves!
They giggled as the waves did sway,
Creating a silly ocean ballet.

So, beneath this canopy wide,
We toasted with seashells, side by side.
With bubbles and laughter in the tide,
In this watery realm, our hearts collide.

Twilight's Embrace on Wistful Shores

The sun winks as it goes away,
The seagulls squawk a cabaret.
A crab in a tux waves me hello,
As I dance with the waves, just so slow.

The sand tickles toes in a giggly spree,
While dolphins prank swim, oh, how they flee!
The beach ball bounced and got stuck in a tree,
Where a parrot shouts, "Free drinks for me!"

Sea shells chatter like gossiping friends,
Confessing tales where the fun never ends.
A fish wearing shades just swam along,
Singing sea shanties in the evening song.

With every splash, a laugh we find,
Even the waves have a silly mind!
So here's to laughter and sandy delight,
And twinkling stars on this joyful night.

Beneath the Riptide's Cloak

Underneath the waves, a treasure chest,
Gems and gold, a pirate's request.
Yet all we find is a fish with a shoe,
Who danced a jig to the ocean's blue.

A clam makes jokes in its bumpy shell,
Telling bad puns that I know too well.
Octopus serves drinks with a spicy flair,
While mermaids gossip and flip their hair.

The seaweed flirts like a playful kiss,
Entangling toes in a watery bliss.
Jellyfish bounce in a gooey parade,
Coming for selfies—their famous charade!

But watch out, my matey, for waves can surprise,
Just like a turtle who giggles and flies.
As we dive deep, we might just get lost,
In the hilarious chaos that the sea has tossed!

Parables of the Deep Blue Sea

Beneath the frothy waves, tales unfold,
Where fishes have stories, and oysters are bold.
A grouper recites Shakespeare with flair,
While crabs crack up, just without a care.

The starfish plays chess with shells as its pals,
Mapping the tides and forgotten gals.
A whale tells the kids about faraway lands,
While everyone giggles and gives their demands.

A clam misplaces its peek-a-boo game,
And all the sea creatures shout in its name!
While dolphins prank call the seagulls nearby,
With silly accents that make everyone cry.

So gather around for the tales set at sea,
With laughter and joy, just like a big spree.
For we're all just voyagers, wild and free,
Living in moments that make spirits glee!

Dreamscapes of the Untamed Water

In a world beneath, where dreams spin round,
A starfish floats, wearing a crown so profound.
With pearls for a throne, it reigns in delight,
While bubbles burst out, causing giggles that night.

An eel tells tales of the world far and wide,
While sea cows cheer and take sides for the ride.
Playful krill form conga lines with bliss,
As tuna join in with a boisterous kiss.

The sea cucumbers dance wasabi tango,
While anchovies gossip, "To swim or to mango?"
Anemones sway to a beat oh so fun,
As otters enact a hilarious run.

So dive into worlds where laughter abounds,
Where even the deep makes the silliest sounds.
In the vastness of waves, let's laugh till we tire,
And float on our dreams, in the moon's gentle fire.

www.ingramcontent.com/pod-product-compliance
Lightning Source LLC
Chambersburg PA
CBHW072215070526
44585CB00015B/1355